# Table of Contents

# Ingredients

3/4 teaspoon ground white pepper

6 boneless chicken breast halves

3 plum tomatoes

1 tablespoon Italian seasoning

3 cups milk

6 tablespoons butter

4 cloves garlic

8 ounces Monterey Jack cheese

3/4 cup grated Parmesan cheese

1 package mushrooms

1 onion

1/3 cup all-purpose flour

1 pound fettuccine pasta

1 cup half-and-half

1 tablespoon salt

# Directions

1. In a medium-sized skillet, add the butter, Italian seasoning, chicken and garlic.
2. When the chicken is cooked, remove it from the skillet and set aside.
3. In a large pot, add the salt and water then bring them to a boil.
4. Once the water is boiling, add the uncooked pasta and cook it until it becomes al dente or its consistency is firm when you bite it.
5. In a large skillet, add butter to sauté the onions, garlic and mushrooms.
6. When the onions turn translucent, slowly add the salt, milk, flour, half-and-half, cheese and pepper; mix all the ingredients until smooth.
7. Add the chicken mixture, sour cream; tomatoes and heat for at least 5 minutes then remove skillet from the heat.
8. Toss the fettuccine pasta to evenly coat it with the Alfredo sauce.
9. Serve on a large plate and garnish it with freshly grated cheese and parsley.

# Classic Fettuccine Alfredo Pasta

# Ingredients

5 cloves garlic

2 cups Parmesan cheese

1 cup heavy cream

2 tablespoons parsley

1 egg yolk

10 ounces fettuccine pasta

1/2 cup butter

# Directions

1. In a large pot, bring salted water to a boil and add the pasta; cook until it becomes al dente, and then drain.
2. Meanwhile, in a medium-sized skillet, add garlic and butter then cook for 3 minute until the garlic turns light brown.
3. In a small bowl, add an egg yolk and heavy cream then mix them well; pour the ingredients in a frying pan.
4. Add the parsley and cheese to the cream mixture and mix until it smoothens.
5. Serve the fettuccine pasta on a large serving plate and pour the Alfredo sauce.
6. Before serving, toss the Classic Fettuccine Pasta with the Alfredo sauce to evenly coat it, and then garnish with parsley.

Please leave a review on Amazon.com.

# Sausage Fettuccine Alfredo

# Ingredients

½ cup + 2 tablespoons Locatelli cheese

1/2 pound sweet Italian sausage

8 ounces fettuccine pasta

1 cup heavy cream

3 tablespoons fresh parsley

1/2 cup butter

# Directions

1. Prepare a deep-bottomed pot and fill it halfway with cold water then add salt.
2. When the salted water is already boiling, add all the 8 ounces of fettuccine pasta and cook for 10 minutes.
3. In a skillet, cook the sausage until it becomes golden brown.
4. When the sausage is done, remove from the skillet and set aside.
5. For the sauce, use a large saucepan and melt the butter then add the cheese and heavy cream.
6. Constantly stir the butter, sausage, Locatelli cheese and heavy cream until you bring it to a soft boil; add the parsley.
7. On a bed of fettuccine pasta, pour the cooked sauce and top the pasta with an additional serving of crumbled sausages.
8. Serve the Sausage Fettuccine Alfredo and enjoy while hot.

Please leave a review on Amazon.com.

# Garlic Fettuccine Alfredo

Total Time: 25 minutes
Preparation Time: 0 minutes
Cooking Time: 25 minutes

# Ingredients

2 tablespoons cream cheese

1 lb. fettuccine pasta

Black pepper

1 pint heavy cream

2/3 cup Parmesan cheese

1/2 cup butter

1 teaspoon garlic powder

Salt

# Directions

1. In a saucepan, melt the butter; add cream cheese, heavy cream, pepper, garlic powder and salt.
2. Simmer the ingredients for 20 minutes and when it is done, add the Parmesan cheese.
3. Once done, get a large clean plate, toss the pasta with the Alfredo sauce and serve it while hot.
4. Garnish with an additional serving of freshly grated Parmesan cheese.

Please leave a review on Amazon.com.

# Bacon Fettuccine Pasta with Chicken Alfredo Sauce

Total Time: 30 minutes

Preparation Time: 4 minutes

Cooking Time: 26 minutes

# Ingredients

1 pound chicken breasts

1 package fettuccine pasta

2 cups fresh mushrooms

1/2 cup Parmesan cheese (for cooking)

8 bacon strips

1 garlic clove

1 teaspoon paprika

6 green onions

1 and 1/2 cups half-and-half cream

1/2 teaspoon ground pepper

¼ cup Parmesan cheese (for garnishing)

# Directions

1. In a large pot, bring water and salt to a boil for 5 minutes.

2. Add the uncooked Fettuccine pasta to the boiling salted water and cook until it turns al dente.

3. Meanwhile, in a skillet, fry the bacon to a crisp then reserve 2 tablespoons of bacon fat then set aside.

4. Transfer the bacon to a paper towel to drain; set aside.

5. In the same skillet, sauté the sliced chicken breasts in bacon fat; stir in green onions and mushrooms.

6. Add the garlic and cook for a minute before adding the cheese, pepper, paprika and cream.

7. Simmer the ingredients for 10 minutes then add the bacon.

8. In a serving bowl, add the drained pasta and toss the Alfredo sauce; evenly coat and season with pepper and salt.

9. Transfer the Bacon Fettuccine Pasta with Chicken Alfredo Sauce on a plate and top it with ¼ cup of freshly grated Parmesan cheese.

Please leave a review on Amazon.com.

# Easy-to-Cook Alfredo Fettuccine

Total Time: 25 minutes

Preparation Time: 15 minutes

Cooking Time: 10 minutes

# Ingredients

1/2 cup milk

1/2 cup butter

8 ounces cream cheese

8 ounces fettuccine

3/4 cup Parmesan cheese

# Directions

1. In a medium-sized pot, bring water and salt to a boil before adding the pasta; cook for 15 minutes.

2. Once the pasta is al dente, drain it in a colander and set aside.

3. In a saucepan, mix the butter, cream cheese, milk and Parmesan cheese.

4. In a serving plate, toss the al dente fettuccine pasta with the Alfredo sauce, coat well and garnish with freshly grated Parmesan cheese.

Please leave a review on Amazon.com.

# Fettuccine Alfredo with Shrimps

# Ingredients

3/4 cup Parmesan cheese

1 tablespoon olive oil

1 tablespoon butter

3 green onions

3/4 lb. medium raw shrimp

1 cup whole milk

Salt

6 garlic cloves

8 ounces fettuccine

1 teaspoon cornstarch

# Directions

1. In a medium-sized pot, add water and pasta; cook for 10 minutes until al dente.
2. Just drain the water when the pasta is done and set aside.
3. In a small bowl, whisk the cornstarch and milk.
4. Meanwhile, in a large skillet, heat butter and oil then add the garlic; cook for 5 minutes.
5. When the garlic is soft enough, transfer it to a plate and mash with a fork.
6. In the same skillet, add onions and shelled shrimps; stir milk mixture.
7. Transfer the pasta to a large plate and pour the creamy Alfredo sauce.
8. Serve the Fettuccine Alfredo with Shrimps, season with pepper and salt then top with grated cheese.

Please leave a review on Amazon.com.

# Shrimps and Scallops Fettuccine Pasta Recipe

# Ingredients

1/4 pound sea scallops

1 small shallot

4 ounces uncooked fettuccine

1/2 cup Parmesan cheese

1 garlic clove

1/4 cup white wine

1 cup half-and-half cream

2 tablespoons olive oil

1/4 pound medium shrimp (raw)

2 tablespoons fresh parsley

1/4 cup chicken broth

1 Roma tomato

# Directions

1. In a medium-sized pot, boil the salted water for about 10 minutes and add the uncooked Fettuccine pasta.

2. When the pasta is done, drain the water from the pot.

3. Use a skillet and sauté the shallots, scallops and shrimps for 5 minutes.

4. Once the ingredients are cooked, add the white wine, chicken broth and garlic then simmer for eight minutes.

5. After eight minutes remove skillet from the heat and set aside.

6. In the same skillet, heat the cream for five minutes then toss in the cooked pasta; return the shrimps and scallops mixture.

7. Serve your homemade Shrimps and Scallops Fettuccine Pasta on a plate; garnish with parsley.

Please leave a review on Amazon.com.

# Fettuccine in Low-Fat Alfredo Sauce

# Ingredients

1 egg yolk

8 ounces fettuccine

1 cup low-fat milk

1/2 teaspoon ground pepper

1/2 cup Parmesan cheese

2 tablespoons butter

1 cup low fat cottage cheese

# Directions

1. In a medium pot, boil water and uncooked Fettuccine noodles until al dente.
2. Meanwhile, in a food processor, combine the egg yolk, milk, pepper and cottage cheese.
3. Transfer the puréed cheese mixture to a saucepan and add butter.
4. After occasionally stirring the mixture, mix in Parmesan cheese and set aside.
5. Once the pasta is cooked, toss it with the Alfredo sauce and serve right away.
6. Garnish the Fettuccine in Low-Fat Alfredo Sauce with extra grated Parmesan cheese.

Please leave a review on Amazon.com.

# Fettuccine Pasta Alfredo with Broccoli Florets

# Ingredients

1/4 cup Parmesan cheese

1 package fettuccine

3 tablespoons butter

1 cup fresh broccoli

2/3 cup milk

1 tablespoon all-purpose flour

Cooking oil

Water